ROME

Designed and Produced by

Ted Smart & David Gibbon

MAYFLOWER BOOKS · NEW YORK CITY

ROME is the 'Eternal' city, yet from any one of the viewpoints of its seven hills one sees magnificent historical buildings that are shedding their stucco, tiled roofs that look as if they might be blown away at the next gale, brick walls that are about to collapse and the ruins of over 2000 years of history that appear to have survived only by a miracle.

To a tidy and logical-minded visitor this state of affairs is most unsettling. 'Why', the visitor asks himself, 'do they not put together all the stones in the Forum into some semblance of order; why are the palazzi not re-stuccoed and painted; why are the narrow alleys through which the traffic weaves at breakneck speed not widened and pavements provided for the pedestrians?'

The answer to the last at any rate is that it was done once and almost everyone agrees that it was a failure. When Mussolini came to an agreement with the Pope over the independence of the Vatican City in 1929 he made a great avenue from the Tiber to St. Peter's, called the Via della Conciliazione. In order to provide space for this great boulevard hundreds of houses had to be demolished. Finally, the avenue up which millions of sightseers and pilgrims make their way every year was built. But few of the Romans liked it; they still don't. They prefer the old narrow streets and the broken-down houses.

Off the broad Via del Corso which stretches north from the Piazza Venezia, and the amazing marble monument to Vittorio Emmanuelle, to the Piazza del Popolo, the streets remain narrow, without pavements and motorists and pedestrians have to make the best of it. Romans would not have it otherwise. The carefully laid out streets of other cities, with special places at which to cross and lights to tell them when to do so, are not for them.

Rome has taken over 2,000 years to build and the building of it has been the product of a continuous process of addition by individuals with diverse opinions. Caesars have built their palaces over those of other Caesars, dukes and bishops have torn down marble and sculptures from old buildings to adorn their own new ones, and the ordinary man in the street has taken what was left to put round his front door or to decorate his garden. When there was nothing left that anyone wanted the Romans turned their back on the remains, as they did with the Forum which, until the eighteenth-century interest in ancient Rome awakened, was just a marshy meadow only suitable for pasturing cows. It was even called the Campo Vaccino or Field of Cattle.

What this means, and it opens a window on the Roman character, is that Romans do not deeply care about preserving ruins for their own sake. Romans, in fact, are much more interested in getting on with their lives in their own way and letting the past and future look after themselves.

There may be city planners in Rome whose fingers are itching to tear down the palazzi, rebuild the Roman ruins and open up streets and roundabouts but if there are they keep a low profile. For if there were any large scale changes to be made in some rational and comprehensive planning scheme the Romans would have something to say about it.

To the Romans the idea of removing the familiar landmarks of their city is intolerable. They are proud of them not simply for what they represent but because they are a part of their own identity, an environment in which each Roman grows up and which provides him with a sense of continuity and reassurance of life. To this extent Rome is Eternal; in the bric-a-brac of the past is continuity and it is the chain of life that binds the people of Rome through the centuries.

Romans are fascinated by people. At any time of the day or night you will find them sitting in cafés, on the steps of public buildings, or any surface which can be used for sitting or leaning on and they will be watching other Romans or possibly the tourists from abroad.

One can imagine the same spectators in the Forum of Ancient Rome, watching the manners and gestures of the senators, sizing them up. And watching the barbarians when they arrived with their cavalry, or the ill-behaved sons of the squirearchy on the Grand Tour, or the German and the American soldiers in more recent times.

Centuries of observation of the human comedy and their acquired experience of human behaviour have had a curious effect on the Romans. They appear to express their feelings readily, they wear their hearts on their sleeves. Or do they? Are not the gestures and facial expressions a stylization of reaction, like masks in Greek drama, and is not the reality of emotion and thought hidden even more subtly than by not expressing it at all? Perhaps that is why the Romans are so intent while conversing; one watches the other act out a part, then the roles are reversed. What is behind the tragic gesture, the hopeless shrug, the boast and the promise?

The most popular and comfortable places in which Romans observe each other are the restaurants. So here also they are most on their guard. They arrive and select a table and look at the menu and discuss it with the waiter according to the accepted style. Polished, knowledgeable, presenting a smooth manner to the rest of the world, they try to preserve 'la bella figura', to make a good impression. But as the evening goes on the guard comes down and everyone can enjoy themselves with their own party while at the same time watching others. Perhaps that is why restaurants in Rome are often still full of people and conversation and animation after midnight.

Rome, then, is fundamentally people in a setting

of the buildings left behind by Romans over centuries and centuries. The people will vary a little from place to place, but not essentially. In the Via del Corso, for instance, there is the Piazza Colonna, which takes its name from the huge column of Marcus Aurelius which stands on a pedestal in its center. It is a small square, near the Chamber of Deputies and the Stock Exchange. Traditionally, this is the center of Rome and all day and during the evening it is a gathering place for groups of men discussing business in much the same way as the ancient Romans did in the Forum. The men may look intent, serious, concentrating on their business discussions, but they are no more so than the ladies at the Piazza Vittorio Emmanuelle II near the railway station. Here another kind of business is transacted; the no less serious one of buying food. The market spreads all round the largest square surrounded by nineteenth century houses. Boxes of fish: tunny, sardines, bass, red mullet, conger, squid, octopus and shellfish glisten in the sun, and every now and again the stall holders throw a bucket of water over them to maintain their fresh appearance. Freshness is an important quality to the Roman housewife, so is ripeness and plumpness. She prods the live chickens attached to a rail with a thoughtful finger and finally picks one she likes. The stallholder swiftly decapitates it and puts it headfirst into a funnel from which its legs jerk briefly as its blood runs out into a bucket. The stallholder assures his customer that she has made a good choice, she nods gravely and the transaction is concluded.

Similar scenes were common in the old Roman center of the city, but the Forum now only survives as a market for antiquity. Around its perimeter the stalls are full of resin replicas of monuments and statues of the past, and standing by patiently are the horses and carriages which will transport the visitors on their magic rubber tires to the baths of Caracalla and Nero's Nymphaeum.

During the day the Forum is full of groups of visitors stopping at the spot where Caesar was killed or examining the black stone, the Lapis Niger, which marks the last resting place of Romulus. With apprehension they descend into the interior of the Mamertine prison where the Romans threw the chiefs of conquered tribes after the triumphal march up the Via Sacra. Vercingetorix, the courageous leader of the Gauls, was tortured here and St Peter imprisoned before being beheaded.

They were a ruthless lot, the creators of the grandeur that was Rome, and as dangerous to each other as to their enemies. On the Palatine Hill their palaces lie one upon the other like the corpses of their own family dynasties. Pompey destroyed by Caesar, Caesar by Brutus and Cassius, they in turn by Octavius and Mark Antony who, with his mistress Cleopatra, was later eliminated by Octavius, the great Augustus Caesar, who was followed by a succession of power-bemused tyrants: Tiberius, Caligula, Nero, Domitian. Among them there were a few wiser ones like Marcus Aurelius or Hadrian, but most would prove the dictum that power corrupts.

But it was also their power that bequeathed to Rome its great monuments. Augustus Caesar built the Theater of Marcellus down towards the Tiber and its only island, the Ara Pacis, and the Forum of Augustus; Tiberius built the Temple of Augustus and rebuilt the Temple of Castor and Pollux whose three columns grace the center of the Forum: Hadrian built the great Mausoleum which is now known as the Castel Sant'Angelo.

Though the ghosts of early Romans haunt most of the city, the buildings one sees came later. Those huge palazzi with their shuttered windows, and tall entrance doors, the solid walls of houses in the narrow streets, are the work of the sixteenth, seventeenth and eighteenth centuries. The quarter between the Via del Corso and the Tiber evokes this period wonderfully. The streets are narrow and twist and turn between the monuments of Rome and the Renaissance. Near its center lies the Pantheon, the best preserved Roman temple, and near it the Church of Santa Maria di Minerva which illustrates the way in which the city's architecture has evolved. Built in the thirteenth century and modelled on the Florentine church of Santa Maria Novella it was turned into a classical structure by Maderno, who also redesigned the front of St Peter's. In the nineteenth century, however, its medieval style was reintroduced.

Also in this area is one of the great social gathering places of Rome, the Piazza Navona, a long rectangular space whose shape betrays its origin as a Circus built by Domitian. Three fountains provide focus points for the children who play in the square watched by their families, and cafés along the fronts of the houses provide seats from which spectators can watch one of the most animated squares in the city.

North-west of the Corso is a social center of another kind. Here in the streets with names like Via Condotti, Borgognone and Frattini there is a relatively traffic-free area at night where Romans can indulge in their evening 'passegiata', or stroll. This is more than just a means of taking exercise. It is an opportunity to meet and talk with friends looking at the windows of the smart shops with names like Gucci, Ferragamo, Spagnoli or Valentino, or to sit at a café like the famous Café Greco which was the meeting place of noted writers and artists of the nineteenth century.

To the north of these streets lies the famous Piazza di Spagna with its great stone steps surging up from Bernini's boat-shaped fountain to the church of Santa Trinità del Monte. This utterly delightful spot where Keats and Mendelssohn lived has become a focal point for tourist Rome. The steps are crowded with young denim-clad vendors of cheap jewelry and leather belts, lightning sketch artists and musicians who add to the color given to the steps by the flower stalls that line the lower pavement. From above there is a glorious view of the city over tiled roof tops and roof top terraces where little gardens flourish, to the Vatican City.

St Peter's, though the largest church in Christendom is not, however, as many people imagine, the cathedral of the Catholic world nor even of Rome, that honor belongs to the Church of St John Lateran. Popes were crowned here until 1870 when the Popes retreated to the Vatican after the defeat of the papal forces by Garibaldi and the unification of Italy. The Popes remained in the seclusion of the Vatican City until 1929 when a Treaty of Conciliation was signed with Mussolini.

In the terms of the Treaty St John Lateran was granted extraterritorial rights with the Churches of Santa Maria Maggiore and San Paolo Fuori le Mura.

St John Lateran lies at the very gates of Rome by the Porta San Giovanni and the beginning of the Appian Way, one of the most evocative of the Roman roads leading out of Rome, especially in the early morning or late evening when the traffic has diminished and the sun's rays are slanting across the land casting long shadows of the pines and tombs that line the road across the worn Roman paving stones.

South of the walls of the city there is a different picture of Rome from that of the smart residential streets off the Via Veneto which leads to the Porta Pinciana. Here are the quarters of the working people of Rome where small houses abound and the evidence of Roman domestic life is visible. Further west towards the Tiber is the Gate of San Paolo, by which one is surprised to see a pyramid. This was erected by a Roman, Gaius Cestius who, though of little importance to posterity, was honored for his services to his contemporaries as the man in charge of important banquets. Also at this gate is the Protestant cemetery where John Keats is buried under a stone which bears the famous lines, 'Here lies one whose fame is writ in water'. A modest claim in a city which does not go in for understatement. Humility is something else however and one of the cardinal virtues of the Church whose domains lie across the Tiber.

The independent sovereign state of the Vatican which once held sway over Tuscany, Umbria and many other parts of Italy and still reigns over the religious life of more than 600 million of the world's population, is contained in 108 acres. Though part of Rome, it is literally and spiritually a world apart. The people who throng its great antechamber, the Piazza San Pietro with its colonnades by Bernini, and the huge space before St Peter's Cathedral itself, come from every corner of the earth. The spectacle is overwhelming not only architecturally, but in terms of the people of such a variety of races who slowly approach the magnificent cathedral built, not before some typically Roman arguments, by Bramante, Raphael, Sangallo, Michelangelo and Maderno over a period of more than 130 years.

During the centuries of its great growth to power the Catholic church was allied to all the ruling houses of Italy, to such an extent that it is difficult to separate its spiritual from its secular authority. The Borgias are the family that most people will associate with the Papacy but a glance at a list of Popes soon reveal other connections. Julius II, the instigator of the rebuilding of St Peter's was a della Rovere; Clement VII a Barberini – all of them names associated with families engaged in successful commercial ventures.

Today, the great partnerships between Church and commerce has diminished but the Vatican City remains as solid and eternal as Rome itself. On one of those warm Roman evenings looking across Rome from the Janiculum Hill which stretches south from the Vatican, the city seems covered in a golden veil. The heat haze rises over the rooftops of the Trastevere quarter below where the working population of Rome resides and where restaurants providing tourists with a typical traditional Roman welcome go their boisterous and successful way. Here and there the domes and campaniles of the ancient city rise above the untidy rooftops, in the streets the cars flow like a torrent of steel and in the squares and traffic-free streets the Romans take their evening passegiata. Despite the bustle, a veil of tranquility seems to hang over the city. It is as if time has stopped, as if the whole of history is here in the present and at such a moment it is easy to believe that Rome is eternal, a permanent exposition of past and present gathering the futur in its timelessness.

The eighteenth century preoccupation with a scientific and reasonable explanation of natural phenomena led naturally to an interest in the origins of civilization. How had European civilization arrived where it had and what was its ancestry? The answer was at hand in the buried ruins of the Roman Empire which until then no one had deemed worthy of interest except as a source of free building materials.

As the excavation and restoration of ancient Rome began, and the splendid works of art come to light, the writers and poets and musicians who were the voice of the Romanticism that was beginning to sweep Europe hastened to Italy to draw inspiration from the ruins. Most of them saw the city through the lens of their subjectivism and ancient Rome took on the aspect of a golden age while Rome after Augustus became a symbol of decadence.

The diarist Evelyn, a contemporary of Pepys, was among the first to explore ancient Rome at the time when the Grand Tour was becoming the essential finale to the education of anyone who aspired to culture.

At the beginning of the eighteenth century there was no question of tourist amenities and anyone who wanted to see the relics of antiquity often had to suffer some inconvenience to do so. Evelyn describes his visit to the catacombs, 'Here, in a cornfield, guided by two torches we crept on our bellies into a little hole, about twenty paces, which delivered us into a large entry that led us into several streets or alleys a good depth in the bowels of the earth'.

These newly discovered relics of ancient Rome set artists' minds aflame and no one more than Goethe, the great German playwright and poet. He made two major visits to Rome, being especially impressed by the Circus of Caracalla, the Appian tombs and, like most visitors, the Colosseum. 'Once it has been seen everything else seems small', he said.

Goethe, as a true Romantic, valued a close kinship with nature and he finds this relationship strong among the Italians. 'All I can say about the Italians', he says, 'is this: they are children of Nature, who for all the pomp and circumstance of their religion and art, are not a whit different from what they would be if they were still living in forests and caves'.

One cannot help feeling that Goethe was being carried away by the tendency, common to many of the bourgeois tourists of the nineteenth century, to regard the poverty and squalor, the ragged, barefoot children and the work-worn peasant as picturesque examples of man's eternal struggle with nature.

No doubt he too sent off the popular postcards of the time depicting street scenes in the style of Murillo; poor children with caged birds, or eating water melons; women drawing water from wells and other genre subjects.

Not unexpectedly Charles Dickens, who was a dedicated crusader against the social conditions of his time, took an opposite view. Regarding Rome as not very different from London lying 'under a thick cloud with innumerable towers and steeples and roofs of houses, rising up into the sky, and high above them all, a Dome'.

If he were alive today he could hardly say the same, for Rome has preserved its buildings while London has suffered from the developers' demolition squads and high rise planners.

William Hazlitt had already complained about Roman squalor before Dickens' visit. 'It is not the contrast of pigstys and palaces that I complain of, the distinction between old and new; what I object to is the want of any such striking contrast but an almost uninterrupted succession of narrow vulgar looking streets where the smell of garlick prevails over the odor of antiquity...'

Like most writers on travel, faced with the fact of having to capture their readers' attention with a subject matter that does not lend itself to gripping prose, Hazlitt and Dickens were picking on one aspect of the city, like Mark Twain later who complained that everything was by Michelangelo. No doubt they found many readers to agree with them, but the most powerful effect of Rome on all visitors was from its newly excavated antiquity.

All the artists and writers of the Romantic period visited or lived in Rome during the nineteenth century and for many the city became the core of a life experience which inspired key works.

The most directly influenced was Edward Gibbon whose greatest work was devoted to a study of the historical phenomenon that was the Roman Empire. 'It was at Rome, on 15th October 1764', he says, with the precision of someone who has had a revelation, 'as I sat musing amidst the ruins of the capitol, while the barefooted friars were singing vespers in the Temple of Jupiter, that the idea of writing the decline and fall of the city, first started in my mind'.

Gibbon may not be read much today except by scholars but another group of writers who are widely known were also profoundly affected by Roman antiquity. One of these was Lord Byron, who arrived in 1817 and stayed at the Piazza di Spagna and was a frequenter of the Cafe Greco in Via Condotti which was patronized by artists and musicians including Wagner and Liszt.

Rome to Byron meant another Canto and to posterity the famous lines about the Roman games 'Butchered to make a Roman holiday'.

In a far less melodramatic manner both Shelley and Keats drew inspiration from ancient Rome. Shelley wrote the tragedy of the Cenci while living at Via del corso 375 and suffered tragedy in his own life when his son died. Tragedy is in a sense the companion of Romanticism and John Keats' death at Piazza di Spagna, in a house that is today a memorial museum to both poets, adds poignancy to the story of Rome's ability to stir the imagination of artists and writers.

Both Keats and Shelley and his son are buried at the Protestant cemetery along with countless others for whom Rome was the key to the continuity of the human adventure, and who, too, in the words of Shelley's epitaph, 'suffered a sea change into something rich and strange'.

After the ancient Romans, the most powerful influence in the development and character of the city of Rome has been that of the Pope. Having established their authority in a Europe torn by wars between rival peoples, the Popes were able to come to terms with the ruling dynasties by offering divine blessing and cultural endowment in exchange for military protection.

For the new kings such as Pepin of France, who had usurped the Merovingian throne from his weakling sovereign, the Papal blessing provided the authority he required to establish himself in the minds of his people. Charlemagne, the son of Pepin, protected the Papacy against the Lombards and in return was crowned

Emperor at Pavia by the Pope.

Thus began a partnership between Popes and Emperors which was of mutual benefit and for the first time since ancient Rome the idea of a European Empire was revived. This time, however, it was to be a Holy Roman Empire. There followed a period of growth and commercial prosperity which quickly led to the rebuilding of Europe. It also brought more internal dissension between small and larger powers.

The major area of conflict between the Popes and the Emperors was over who should appoint the bishops who were the virtual rulers of the land that surrounded the monasteries. Henry IV of Germany defied Pope Gregory and was excommunicated. He then invaded Rome and deposed the Pope but in the ensuing struggle Papal authority won the day and the unhappy Emperor was obliged to kneel in the snow outside Canossa for three days awaiting the Papal pardon. From that time few rulers or states attempted to rule without Church support.

The dividing line between the religious and secular worlds now tended to disappear and the Popes became landlords of enormous estates while commercial families fought each other to place one of their relatives on the throne of St Peter. Among them, the Borgias were a supreme example of the art of combining ruthless military power with the authority of divine rule. It was Pope Julius II, who, in succeeding the Borgias, was most influential in giving Papal authority the outward symbols of great power. He decreed that a new church should replace the old basilica built over the grave of St Peter, and commissioned the architect Bramente to plan the work. The great new building took over a hundred years to complete and a variety of architects and artists, including Michelangelo, were involved. Julius II began the collection of statuary housed in the Vatican Palace Museums, he founded the Swiss Guard, and it was he who commissioned Michelangelo to decorate the ceiling of the Sistine Chapel.

The Vatican was only the focal point of the power of the Church and its supporters. All over Rome, palaces sprang up demonstrating the power and the magnificent life style of the Papal princes.

The Orsini built themselves a palace within the remaining arc of the ruins of the Theater of Marcellus. The solid masonry of the outer walls provided protection against any enemies strong enough to get past their mercenary troops commanded by hired condottiere.

The Palazzo di Venezia was built by Cardinal Barbo, later Paul II, a friend of Rodrigo Borgia, and combines the characteristics of a castle with those of a palace. It was here, near the center of Rome overlooking Piazza Venezia, that Mussolini had his offices.

Across the Corso lies another stately pile, the Palazzo Doria Pamphili. The Doria family was descended from the famous Admiral who beat the Turks at the battle of Lepanto, and among the members of the Pamphili family was Pope Innocent X. The palace is open to the public and has a magnificent art collection which includes a picture of the Pope by Velasquez.

Another palace full of works of art is the Palazzo Barberini, near the Piazza of the same name. It was here that Galileo was kept prisoner during his well-known tussle with the Church. Then there is the Palazzo Farnese built by the Cardinal whose sister was the mistress of Pope Alexander VI.

The greatest of the palaces was that of the Vatican itself and today's visitors, strolling through the seemingly endless galleries and courtyards, need little prompting to imagine them full, not of statues, but of the cardinals and ambassadors who were the political negotiators of the Renaissance. The halls were decorated by the finest artists of the period: Raphael, Michelangelo and Leonardo all contributed to the work of beautifying the buildings and the courtyards and magnificent gardens were filled with statues and fountains. The Pope's private chapel, the Sistine, was and still is a wonder of the world. This lavish display was a symbol of Papal power which was both spiritual and temporal.

Today, Papal power exercised through the Vatican and the great Roman families that were allied to it is still something to be reckoned with, though now it operates without public show. The investments of the Vatican Treasury are handled by special administrators and no documents less than a hundred years old are allowed to be examined.

Whatever the material basis of the power of the Roman Catholic Church, there is no doubt about its spiritual hold on the 600 million Catholics in the world and the countless others who are driven by curiosity or a genuine but unformulated spiritual need to visit the Church of St Peter.

One has only to be there on a Sunday for the Papal blessing or on one of the other occasions when the Vicar of Christ addresses the vast crowds assembled in the Piazza before St Peter's to acknowledge that the power that the Pope represents is more than a matter of financial muscle and that its basis is firmly in the conviction of millions of people that the greatest wealth of the Catholic Church is its position at the head of the new society founded by Christ.

Faced with the impressive architecture and the treasures that the Vatican City contains, most visitors find it difficult to remember that the founders of Christianity were a minority with neither power, money nor authority. Nor were they conformists, supporting the ruling establishment of their day; they were rebels whose faith was a threat to those who held power. Some of the most interesting relics of ancient

Rome are those associated with the early Christians.

At first, the Romans regarded the Christians as a small but troublesome minority that needed to be disciplined. Having crucified their leader, an event so insignificant to them that they did not even record it, they forgot about them until Peter arrived in Rome and made himself a nuisance. At first he was put in jail in the Mamertine Prison, the remains of which can still be seen by the Capitoline Hill. Here, he baptized his jailers with water from a spring. To the Romans, already beset with the knowledge that their civilization was breaking down, Peter's new ideas seemed too disruptive, so they executed him at Nero's Circus where he was buried.

Recent excavations under St Peter's have found, amid the mausoleums of the first century necropolis, an empty tomb and, nearby, the bones of a large man, and a series of invocations to St Peter scratched on a retaining wall. It appears therefore that when the Emperor Constantine accepted Christianity and erected the first basilica of St Peter he may have had good reason for choosing the site he did.

The fates of St Paul and St John were the same as that of the first leader of the Christians. They, too, had come to Rome, the center of the world, to preach the new philosophy. Their house, which can be seen under the Church of Santi Giovanni e Paolo, in the park behind the Colosseum, was a two-story one with about twenty rooms and next to a nymphaeum and a palace. Although they were both Romans, the disciples, too, were martyred by Julian the Apostate.

Roman fears of the new ideas grew as their own confidence in the Roman system waned. Like most frightened people, they began to look around for scapegoats to explain their own failure, and chose the Christians.

To protect themselves from persecution the Christians went underground. They dug catacombs in which to bury their dead and for meetings. Many of these can be seen in Rome today, most of them near the Appian Way which was also a favourite burial ground for well-to-do Romans.

The catacombs consisted of a series of underground passages arranged in tiers, sometimes five deep, with niches cut into the walls for the burial of the dead. The bodies were dressed and often carried personal belongings with them. Though the apertures were sealed, grave robbers still broke into the graves to rob the dead of their possessions.

At San Callisto, one of the most important of the catacombs, paintings made on the walls are still visible. Most of them relate the stories of the Old Testament, and the symbol for Christ, a fish, appears frequently.

There are many catacombs in the area, including some used by the Jews. These were excavated in 1857, and the seven-branched candlestick was one of the symbols most frequently found.

Death and persecution seem to haunt this part of Rome, for not far away is the spot where the Germans shot 335 Italians in reprisal for an attack on German soldiers in Rome during the second World War. The unhappy victims were buried in a mass grave, now known as the Mausoleo delle Fose Ardeatine.

In the Via delle Sette Chiese, the street of the seven pilgrimage churches, are the catacombs of St Domitilia, who was a niece of the Emperor Domitian's sister.

The Christians, whose beliefs became more and more unacceptable to Rome, suffered increasingly as the problems of the Empire defied solution. At the same time the miraculous events associated with the Christian Saints multiplied. St Agnes, after whom the Church in Piazza Navona is named, was exposed naked in Domitian's Circus, but a sudden and miraculous growth of hair saved her modesty. The chains that had bound St Peter suddenly came together when the two pieces, one from Constantinople and the other from Rome, were placed in the Church of San Pietro in Vincoli; and the Virgin Mary appeared to Pope Liberius and told him to build the Church of Santa Maria Maggiore.

Although the persecution of Christians continued, despite such miracles, the new movement grew until the rulers of Rome began to see that it could become the force that might hold together the disintegrating Empire. The Emperor Constantine proclaimed freedom of worship in 313 and this was followed by a wave of church building as the Christians openly celebrated the triumph of their faith.

Among the churches built in the fourth century were Santa Maria in Trastevere, Sant'Alessio and Santa Prisca on the Aventine across the river, also San Clemente and Sant'Agnese Fuori le Mura. St John Lateran was begun and also San Paolo Fouri le Mura and Santa Croce in Gerusalemme, built by Constantine to enshrine the relics of the True Cross.

Many of the original buildings have collapsed, or have been built over by later structures. Among the latter, recent excavations have revealed the existence of Mithraic temples on which the first Christian buildings were erected. San Clemente is one of these and so is Sant'Agnese and in their damp and sunken interiors the visitor is reminded forcibly of the beginnings of a philosophy that overturned the Roman World and opened up new avenues of thought for the human race.

Christian saints and pagan gods live side by side in Rome, each representing the dual nature of the city itself. On the one hand is the intellectual and materialist world of modern European man, and on the other the ancient universal pantheism that underlies all of life.

As it took hold of people's imagination Christianity absorbed pagan gods and beliefs, transforming them into Christian saints and rituals. But in the unconscious levels of the mind the pagan spirit lived on; in Rome it can be seen expressed in the statues surrounding the many fountains that give Romans a refuge and haven of coolness even on the hottest days.

For many people, the most attractive of the city's many fountains is the Fontana di Trevi, and with good reason. The great scenic spectacle is unrivalled by any city fountain in the world. On a wild landscape of rocks set against the background of a classical building two Tritons guide Neptune's chariot through the waves. The water, first brought to this spot by Agrippa on one of the aqueducts the ancient Romans were so adept at building, gushes abundantly into the basin: seventeen and a half million gallons a day pouring through with a steady roar that almost drowns that of the traffic.

Tradition has it that coins thrown into the fountain will guarantee a return to Rome, and there are few visitors who do not contribute to the haul of those who look after the fountain. Whether the promise is fulfilled or not does not matter. On a summer night, with the fountain floodlit and the green water silhouetting the people gathered round the basin and the old houses crowding round the square, one coin is a small price to pay for so much splendor.

A Triton is also the subject of Bernini's lovely fountain in the Piazza Barberini. This one is sitting on a huge shell supported by dolphins and from the conch held in his hand the water pours out, fresh and clear, making a sparkling contrast to the dusty buildings round about. Nearby is another Bernini fountain but without pagan connotations; this one features a bee, the symbol of the house of Barberini.

Female companions of the watery gods are naiads, and these nymphs sport in the waters of the fountain at the Piazza della Republica. Romans still call this piazza by its old name of Esedra, which is derived from the Latin for entrance hall. It was in fact the entrance to the baths of Diocletian, the restored ruins of which are still standing and house the National Museum. Diocletian's baths, the largest in Rome, could accommodate over 3,000 people and received their water supply through the aqueduct built by Claudius, which has also been restored.

Gods of the liquid element are commemorated in most of the fountains. This is not surprising since it is due to them that the supply of water is plentiful. Sometimes the gods represent rivers as at the Via delle Quattro Fontane, the charming crossroads where Via del Quirinale and Via XX Settembre meet. The Nile and the Tiber recline in godlike repose at this junction from where one can see three of Rome's famous hills – the Quirinale, the Pincio at Piazza di Spagna and the Esquiline – rising in the distance.

The Nile features again in the Piazza Navona where the central fountain celebrates the four rivers, Danube, Nile, Plate and Ganges. Fountains lie at each end of this most atmospheric piazza, the fountain of the Moor at the northern end, where Tritons surround the figure of a moor and, at the southern end, Neptune battling with a sea monster.

It is curious that so many of these fountains were ordered by Popes who might have been expected to favor Christian themes rather than pagan ones, and Christian figures rather than the muscular nudes that glorify the sensuality of man's nature.

On his return from France in 1814, Pius VII ordered the construction of the Piazza del Popolo at the gate leading out into the Via Flaminia and in each of the elegant crescents of this huge piazza he placed two fountains where Tritons and River gods stand amid the cool waters.

Above the Piazza del Popolo is the Pincio Hill and its wooded parks – a more natural setting for pagan gods, where the ilex trees and olives seem appropriate flora for the rites by which the seasons and all the rhythms of natural life are maintained. The Pincio is a favorite gathering place for Roman families, especially at weekends when the gravel-covered piazza that overlooks the city is full of children enjoying the delights of a small merry-go-round and of the icecream and sweets, balloon and windmill vendors, like employees of Bacchus, encouraging the enjoyment of juvenile sensual pleasures.

Behind the Pincio lies one of Rome's great parks, the Villa Borghese. The Villa was created by Cardinal Scipione Borghese, a man of great taste and a lover of life, like so many of the cardinals of the seventeenth century. Today, the grounds include those of the Villa Giulia, and their 1700 acres include horse riding circuits, ponds, and a zoo. An abundance of trees – oaks, giant ilexes and pines – give it a wild setting. In the evenings, with the rays of the setting sun coloring the leaves gold and casting shadows among the undergrowth, it has a mystery that fits well with the pagan statues that are scattered about the grounds.

But it is in the parts of Rome where ruins decorate the open spaces that the pagan atmosphere is most potent. The painters, Claude Lorrain and Turner, have depicted well those golden distances where the trees and bushes are hidden in a golden mist, and columns, arches and broken walls rise into the clear skies. In them is the continuing memory of a time when nature ruled through mysterious and capricious gods and goddesses and not scientific laws, when a sunset was imbued with deep emotional significance and was not simply a pleasing arrangement of color governed by meteorological phenomena operating according to prescribed laws.

In Rome one feels very much that science is the young man who knows it all but comes to greater wisdom later in life.

Though Romans feel a fierce pride for their city, they also need to get away from it occasionally, and in summer streams of cars are seen every weekend heading for the coast or towards the Alban Hills and lakes. Both of these areas fall into what is known as the Roman Campagna, which stretches from the sea to the hills lying east of Rome and was the land from which all the people of the Italian race originated. The countryside is charming, with olive trees, vineyards, the ruins of aqueducts, and dusty peasant houses whose walls are decorated with drying corn. There is a sense of timelessness about the scene.

By contrast, on the sea coast, the Lidos of Anzio, Fiumicino where Rome airport is situated, and Ostia are modern towns rebuilt after 1945 and crowded with all the modern amenities of a seaside resort. Ostia is now called Lido de Roma, and was once an important Roman port. Nearby Ostia Antica has been excavated and provides a fascinating picture of seafarers, traders and the life of a port in Roman times. Water no longer laps the quayside of ancient Ostia, however, as a great flood in 1557 caused the river entrance to the port to silt up. Instead there are meadows and pine trees surrounding the old warehouses, the three-story villas of the seafaring merchants, and the temples where they propitiated the gods of the sea and the weather.

In the silence of the deserted city it is easy to imagine the life of the port at which the spoils of war and the food that kept the capital city alive were unloaded. Wheat from North Africa, cotton from Egypt, timber from Lebanon and slaves from all the conquered territories, have all landed along the now overgrown quaysides.

The ships that docked at Ostia were heavy Roman triremes driven by slave labor and carrying a simple sail: sea-going ships different from those discovered in the lake at Nemi which lies south west of Rome and which were burned by German soldiers in 1944. Models of the ships and metal decorations remain, however, and give some idea of their splendor. Built by Caligula, they conveyed visitors across the lake for the festival of the goddess Diana.

Argria, the sacred wood in which the goddess resided, was guarded by her priest, who held the title of Rex or King. Any slave who managed to steal a branch of the golden bough, possibly a form of mistletoe, hanging amid the trees, was entitled to challenge the King to mortal combat and become King in his place if he survived. It was the investigation of this strange rite that led Sir James Frazer to write his important and voluminous work 'The Golden Bough'.

Today, the lake which, like others in the Alban Hills, is an old volcanic crater filled with water, is a popular Roman resort. The atmosphere of ancient times clings to it strongly, especially in the evenings when the shadows of the hills creep across the lake and darkness invades its wooded shores.

Nearby is Lake Albano, another popular resort, above which is Castel Gandolfo, the Pope's summer residence. This little town is one of the Castelli Romani, a group of several towns and villages in the Alban Hills which produce celebrated wines, the best-known of which, Frascati, comes from another summer resort almost completely rebuilt since its destruction in the second world war.

The third and most important area outside Rome is the one reached by the Via Tiburtina. This is Tivoli, where the hot springs with their healing properties have attracted Romans both past and present to wooded hills overlooking the Campagna. Around Tivoli the Aniene river cascades through a narrow gorge and almost encircles the town. On a spur of hill which overlooks the valley a circular temple to Vesta still stands. This and another temple to the Sibyl who gave advice to the ancient Roman visitors were converted to Churches during the Middle Ages.

For the modern visitor, the ancient magic still retains much of its potency and Tivoli attracts both foreign tourist and Roman visitor. For the sightseer there is plenty to see, including the famous Villa d'Este with its gardens and fountains.

The greatest marvel of all is not at Tivoli but in the valley below. This is the enormous villa built by the Emperor Hadrian for a retirement that he never fully enjoyed. The villa was designed to include buildings in styles that had impressed Hadrian during his travels abroad. There was to be a vast porch with columns and paintings in imitation of the Stoa Poikile in Athens, a large rectangular pool surrounded by columns and statues like the Canopus in Egypt and a temple in the style of the Temple of Tempe in Thessaly.

Even today, the ruins of this grand concept are impressive. Overgrown with brambles and weeds, the walls of the entrance tower above the flat countryside and in the restored Canopus there is the peaceful haven that Hadrian must have had in mind. The baths, both large and small, are reasonably well preserved and there are many mosaics also in good condition.

As with most Roman buildings, this one was despoiled by barbarians and those who sought its stones and marbles to enrich their own palaces. 'Sic transit gloria mundi' but the vestiges of what is left of the grandeur with which the Romans surrounded themselves even during their leisure provides modern Romans with entertainment in their own excursions from the city that once ruled the world.

There is a famous Roman dish called saltimbocca alla Romana, which, literally translated, means, 'Jump in the mouth in the Roman style'. Like most things Roman this is a bit of hyperbole. Appetizing though it is, the food of the Eternal City is unlikely to launch itself off the plate of its own accord, though it may well be transferred rapidly from dish to mouth by the diner unable to resist its flavor.

Rome is a city full of food shops, markets and restaurants and its citizens pay serious attention to the progress of food from raw material to succulent dish.

The markets are like the overflow of a cornucopia. There are large ones at the Piazza Vittorio Emmanuelle II, at Campo dei Fiori and at Trastevere, and small ones in the side streets of every part of the city. Food is piled high, especially in summer when the fertility of the Campagna and the warmth of the Italian sun provide fruit and vegetables whose dimensions, form and color excite the imagination and arouse the wonder that at other times is stimulated by the noble figures on the Campidoglio or the Bridge of Sant'Angelo.

To the Romans, food of high quality is a natural phenomenon; far from being carried away by the spectacle, they make sure that they select the best of what is available. This situation provides an instant opportunity for communication between stall holders and customers. 'Are the eggs fresh? The meat tender?' 'See signora, feel for yourself, what plumpness! Ripe fruit? Look at this melon. Pure honey'. Arms wave, sincerity is professed, cooking hints exchanged and the seller-customer relationship is strengthened, or not, as the case may be.

In ancient Roman times it was the men who did the shopping, but today the women throng the market places: young wives in jeans and older women in the black dresses that custom used to dictate to the over-thirties.

The stalls are usually covered with a canvas to protect the produce from the sun's rays and there are lights to illuminate the counters during the winter days. At the salumeria stall, strings of salami hang side by side with the round balls of mortadella or bags of ricotta cheese used in making pizza. Dolce latte, gorgonzola and bel paese lie in piles below a glass cover and great wheels of Parmesan are stacked on tables. The fish stalls shine with all the varied produce of the Mediterranean, and mountains of water-melon lie like green cannon balls on the pavement. Some stalls specialize in various kinds of dried pasta in an incredible variety: spaghetti, tagliatelle, ravioli, pasta shaped like shells, others with curled edges, tubular, flat, round, diamond-shaped, some made with wheat flour, others with semolina.

Pasta provides the first steaming plate that calms the appetite in a Roman meal, served either with the traditional Bolognese or Neapolitan sauce, or with Rome's own 'alla matriciana' with pork and tomatoes. Then comes the main dish, perhaps a Roman speciality again, like stufatino, a stew, or agnellino, young lamb.

To accompany the meal, Romans have the wines of the Alban Hills, the best-known of which is probably Frascati. The vineyards in these hills may well have provided wines for the Caesars as they reclined in the gardens of the villas on the Palatine Hill or the countryside round Rome.

Though Romans enjoy meals in the bosom of their family, the habit of going out is also strong, especially during the summer and at weekends when every restaurant is crowded.

Good restaurants abound, particularly those of a down-to-earth variety that concentrate more on the food than on the show business. Luxury restaurants are universal but a good Roman trattoria has a character of its own. The patron or manager will generally assume that his customers are visiting his establishment for his menu and his welcome will often lack the obsequiousness of places where food for the ego is given priority over food for the stomach. He knows, however, that it is his role to be a good host and the entry of a customer is attended by a flurry of activity; crumbs are cleared off tablecloths, menus are flourished and orders for whatever appears to be missing in the table setting are shouted vigorously at the waiters. Once the customer is seated and the order taken, honor has been satisfied and there may be a long wait before the food appears.

Most Romans have habitual eating places which they treat as a second home, a place to entertain their friends or, if they are eating alone, a familiar haven where they can enjoy a good meal and talk to the waiters.

In the tourist quarters some of this homeliness has tended to disappear as the visitors come and go. There is no continuity in the clientele and the restaurant tends to lose some of its life. Fortunately, many restaurants do not change their ways for the tourist and retain the individual characteristics of the proprietor or manager.

This is so even in the eating places in the Trastevere which provide a staged but entertaining evening in the traditional style. This working class part of Rome not only provided gladiators for the Caesars' arenas but also volunteers for the revolutionary army of Garibaldi.

On summer nights, the restaurants spill out into the streets and piazzas and the tables, surrounded by diners under overhead lights round which the moths flutter, seem to float on the dark sea of the pavement. The cool air encourages the appetite and the conversation flows, interrupted only by an occasional musician, until long after midnight. This is the time when eating 'alla Romana' is at its most enjoyable, combining good food and wine with the unending fascination of watching other people.

Italians always think of Rome as being not quite a part of Italy. Rome is where the country is mis-governed, where the money made by the sweat and toil of Italians is mis-spent; it is a community stuck in traditional ways that should long ago have been tossed out of the nearest palazzo window. Strangely enough though, Rome is full of people who have come from

Lombardy and Romagna, and Naples and Sicily, drawn by the possibility of work and the attractions of the big city.

Romans are, in fact, quite like other Italians only more so. The Italian pride in family which puts relatives before national interest has always been strong in Rome; one has only to be aware of the continuing power of the great families, the Orsini, the Chigi, the Borromini, to realise the strength of loyalty. Or think of Napoleon Bonaparte, who was of Italian descent, and remember how he made sure that all his family had the key jobs in his Empire.

Another Italian characteristic which Romans possess to an extreme degree is the desire to impress others. Italians will spend more money than they can really afford on their clothes, ensuring that the label inside their jackets will not humiliate them before their friends. They will order up twelve- or fifteen-course meals for special celebrations; and they find it almost impossible to laugh at a situation that upsets their dignity.

Presenting a 'bella figura', as they call it, is more important to the Romans than to all other Italians. It was a combination of making bella figura and confirming his domestic status that led Julius Caesar to his death. The conspirators played on both these weaknesses and made him change his mind. The same tactics are used today in many every-day negotiations.

Romans have a natural sense of theater: you have only to look at their city to see that. But, unlike the Neapolitans, they act their roles in a classical rather than a Romantic style. They are precise, cool; every gesture is controlled. Whether in the deft laying of a clean cloth on a table, the signals to on-coming traffic, or in the delivery of a political speech, the Roman is a professional.

In his home life, the Roman male is king; at least, that is the way it is made to look to the outsider. His wife looks after his clothes, even to laying them out for him if he is going to an important appointment; she will produce a meal for him at whatever time of the day or night he arrives; she will get the children out of bed if he has a whim to see them; and she will always defer to his superior knowledge even if she knows he is wrong.

For the Roman, the home, and not his work, is the focus of his life. He leaves home in the morning to go to a job but, if he can, he will return there at lunchtime for a meal that his wife has prepared and he will follow that up with a siesta. In the evening after work he will not hurry home, however, but will meet friends in a bar or café, arriving home in time for dinner after eight o'clock.

One of his reasons for keeping out of the way in the evening could well be that his household, like many in Italy, is in reality dominated by women. As well as his wife, there is often a mother or mother-in-law and sometimes unmarried aunts who set the style of life. Most Romans do not necessarily expect to find total communication and satisfaction with the woman they married; they do expect, however, to have a good wife and mother who, like them, will put the family before everything.

The pressures of modern life are changing some of the traditional Roman ways of life. The nature of people's work, the cost of living and the desire for personal freedom may be breaking down the family group but it will take longer in Rome than in some of the industrial cities of the north of Italy where the fragmented life of modern urban civilization is becoming more common.

As a member of the community in which he lives, the Roman is a good citizen. He likes to patronize his local shops and bars, perhaps because they offer the personal relationships with their owners that cannot be established with the staff of the big stores; he often makes an effort to make his balcony or roof terrace attractive by filling them with potted geraniums; he is scrupulously honest and is upset that some Romans and many others who are not Romans live off their wits in the city of tourists.

Although in many ways deeply traditional and conservative, the Roman is also extremely individualistic. He dislikes queuing and when one of the single-decker buses that serve Rome draws up at a stop it is every man, and woman, for him or herself. On the other hand, the Roman will go out of his way to show a stranger how to get across the road or to one of the historical buildings. With over ten million visitors arriving in Rome every year, there are few Romans who are untouched by tourism, but they are less aware of it than the Italians at the seaside resorts.

Romans have seen foreigners come and go throughout their history and though the material well-being of their city has been, and still is being, changed by the arrival of people who come to despoil or increase its wealth, this is not as important to a Roman as the pride which he feels when he says, as did the ancient Romans themselves, 'Civis Romanus Sum'.

Glimpsed through the massive columns of the Temple of Venus and Rome is the Colosseum right, the gigantic amphitheatre that is the largest monument of ancient Rome.

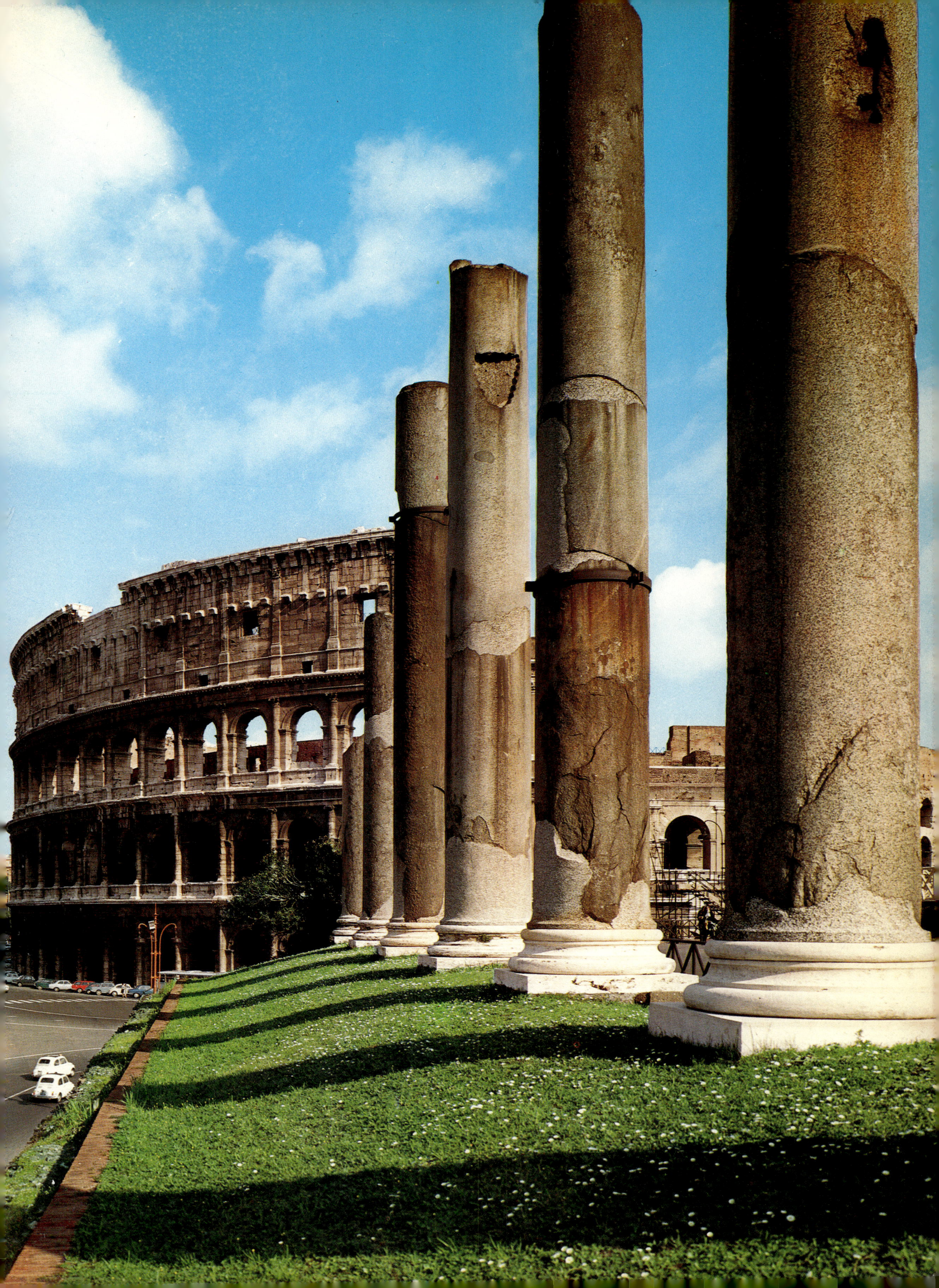

18

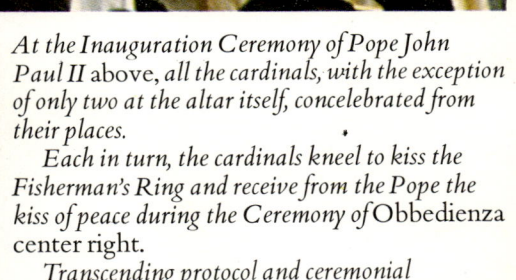

At the Inauguration Ceremony of Pope John Paul II above, all the cardinals, with the exception of only two at the altar itself, concelebrated from their places.

Each in turn, the cardinals kneel to kiss the Fisherman's Ring and receive from the Pope the kiss of peace during the Ceremony of Obbedienza center right.

Transcending protocol and ceremonial distinctions, whether in St. Peter's Square during a General Audience, or in one of the parishes as Bishop of Rome, Pope John Paul II has won the hearts of the people.

19

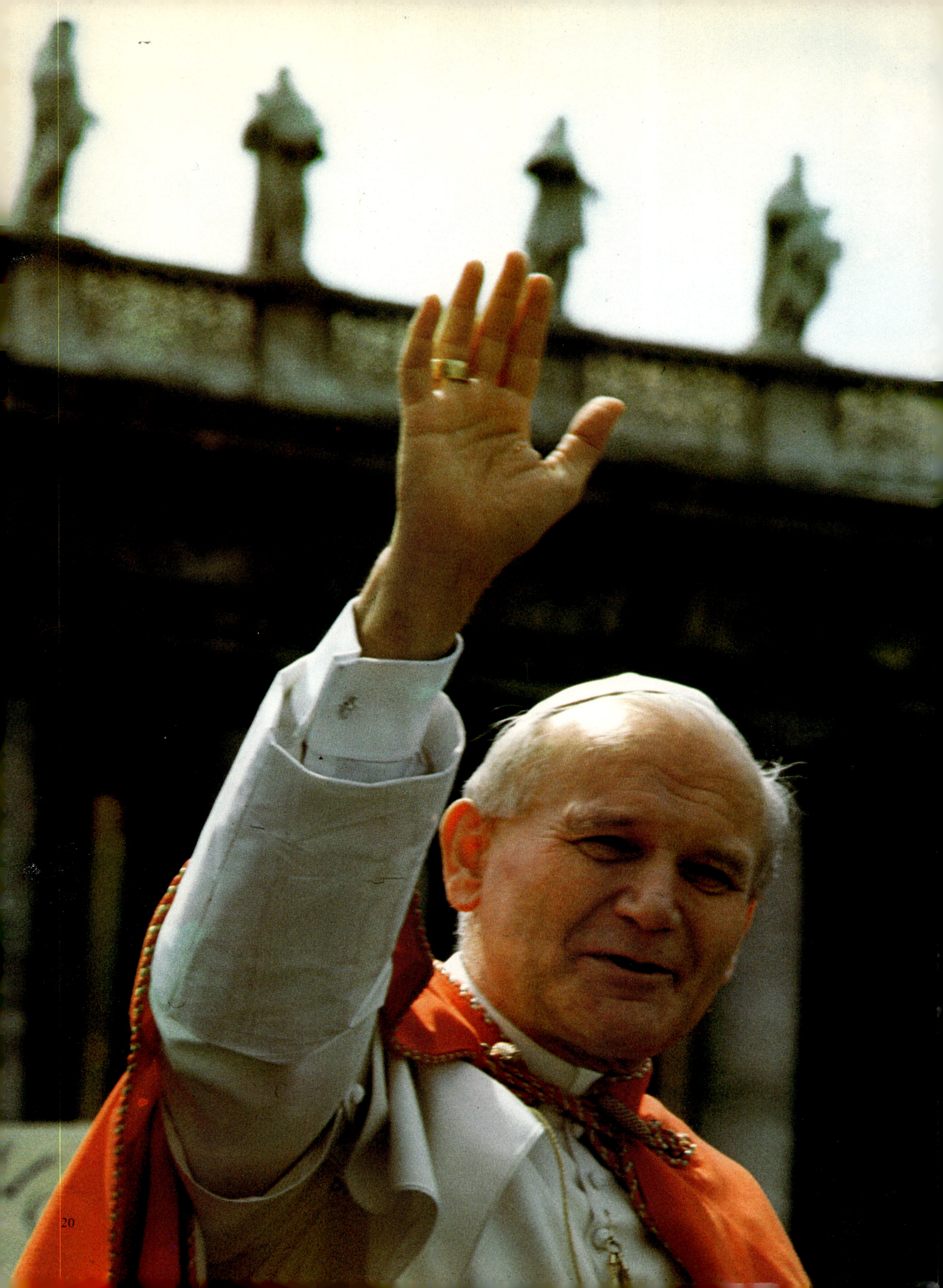

To hear and acclaim the Pope, as Head of the Roman Catholic Church, is the ultimate goal for an endless stream of pilgrims who ceaselessly flock to the Vatican City overleaf, and for those who steadfastly thronged the square awaiting news of the election, on the evening of Monday, 16th October, 1978, their vigil was rewarded when the new Pope, John Paul II, stepped onto the balcony top to a tumultuous reception.

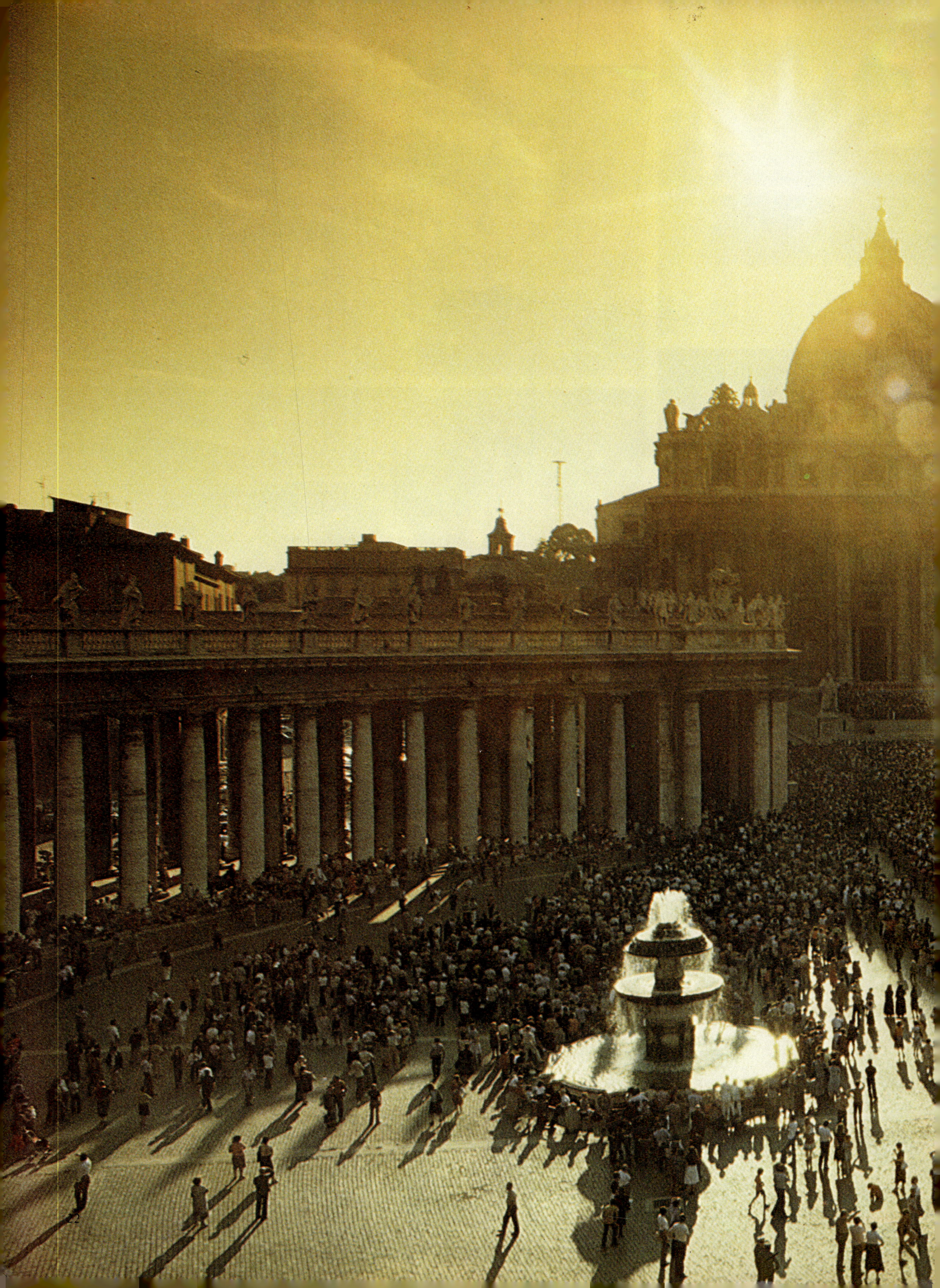

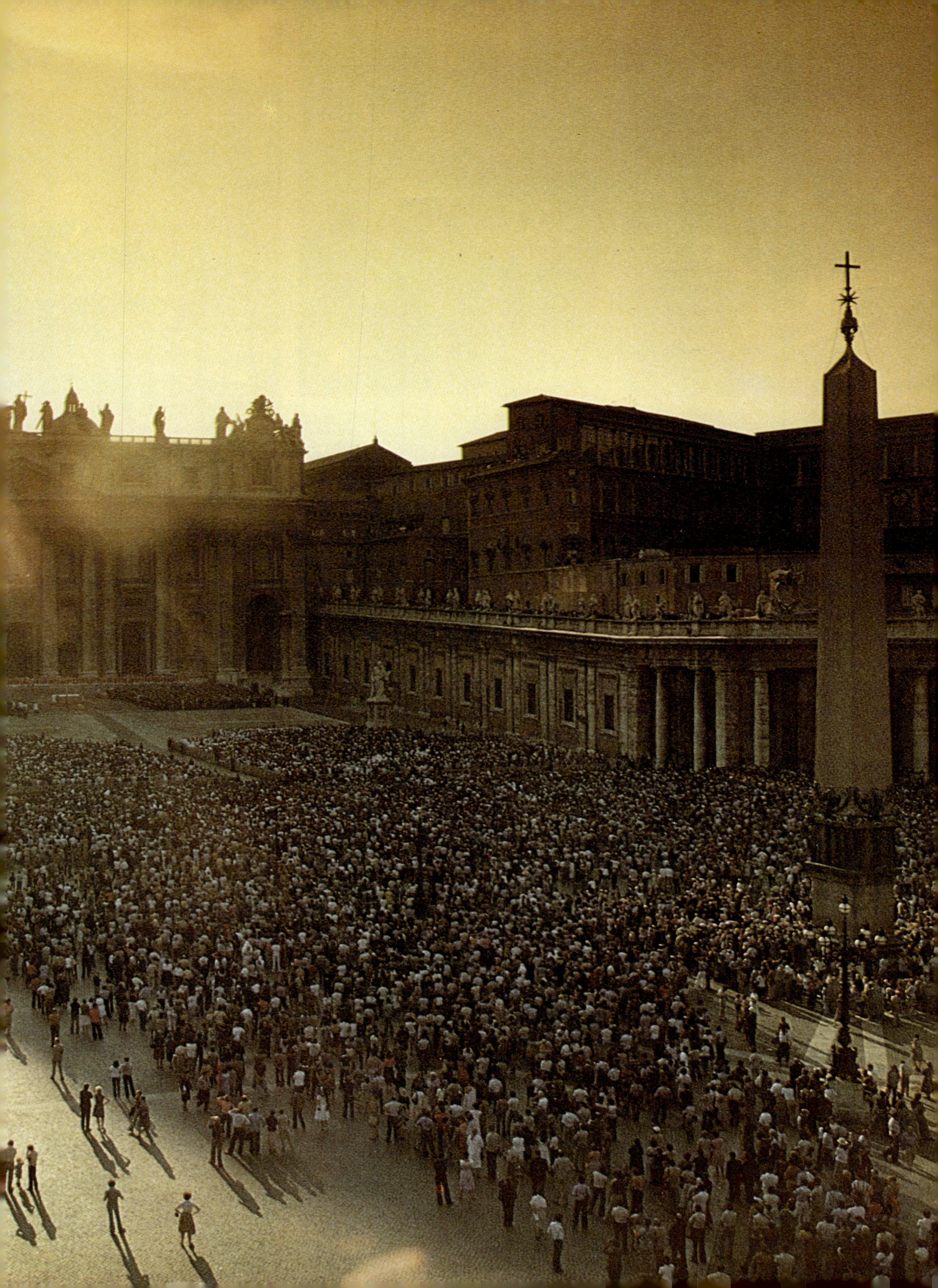

The Vatican Museums, filled with countless treasures and priceless works of art, contain a monumental collection of some of the world's most gifted artistic creators. Top left *is shown the incomparable Sistine Chapel;* center left *the Gallery of Maps;* above *the Gallery of Statues, and* bottom left *the Chiaramonti Museum with its famous sculpture group, "The Nile"* right. Below *can be seen one of the colorfully costumed Swiss Guards who also serve as sentries for palace entranceways in addition to forming the pontiff's personal bodyguard.*

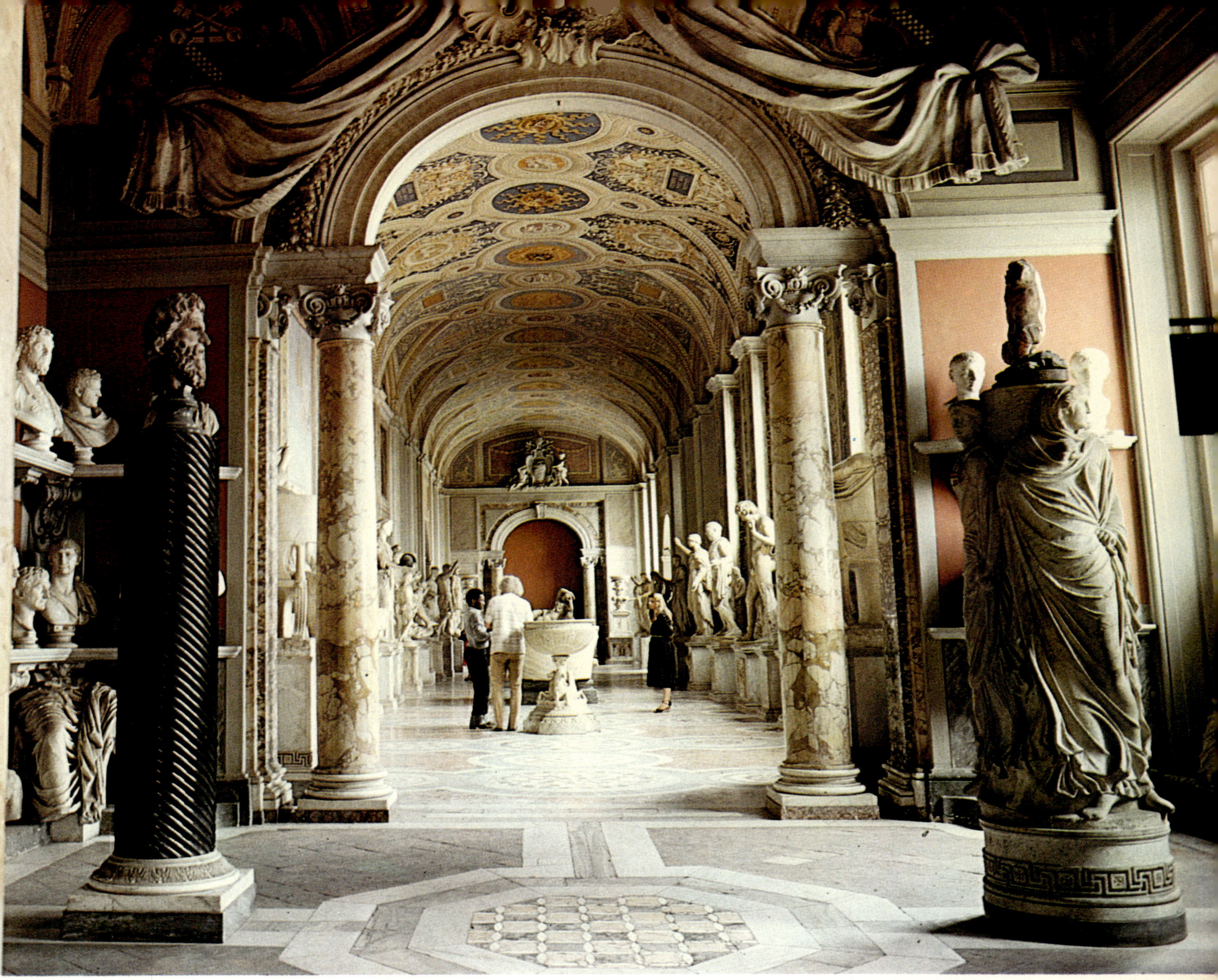

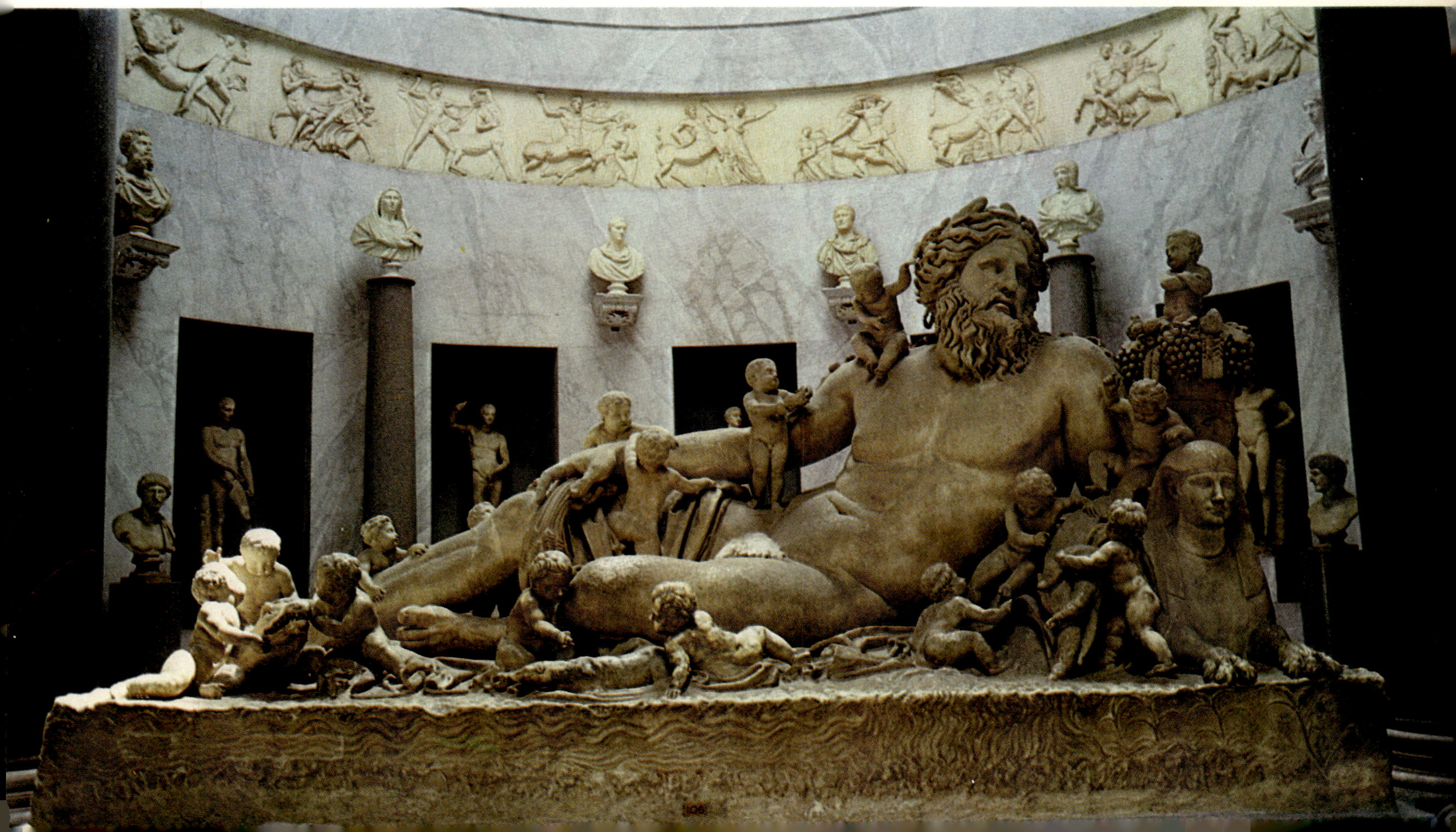

TAXI

bravo
PHOTO
ASSASSINAT
DIMAGRIRE
POPSTEP
QUATTRORUOTE
TUTTO uncinetto
L'Espresso
RAKAM
nautica
milleidee
milleidee
UN LIBRO IN REGALO
UN LIBRO IN REGALO
DA OGGI IN EDICOLA
DoveVa
NUDO E BELLO!
Tuttomoto
GIUGNO
QUATTRORUOTE
ANTEPRIMA
FIDARSI DEI RIPARATORI
EVA EXPRESS
GIOIA
il fisco
ASSASSINATA!
...giocando, il destino...

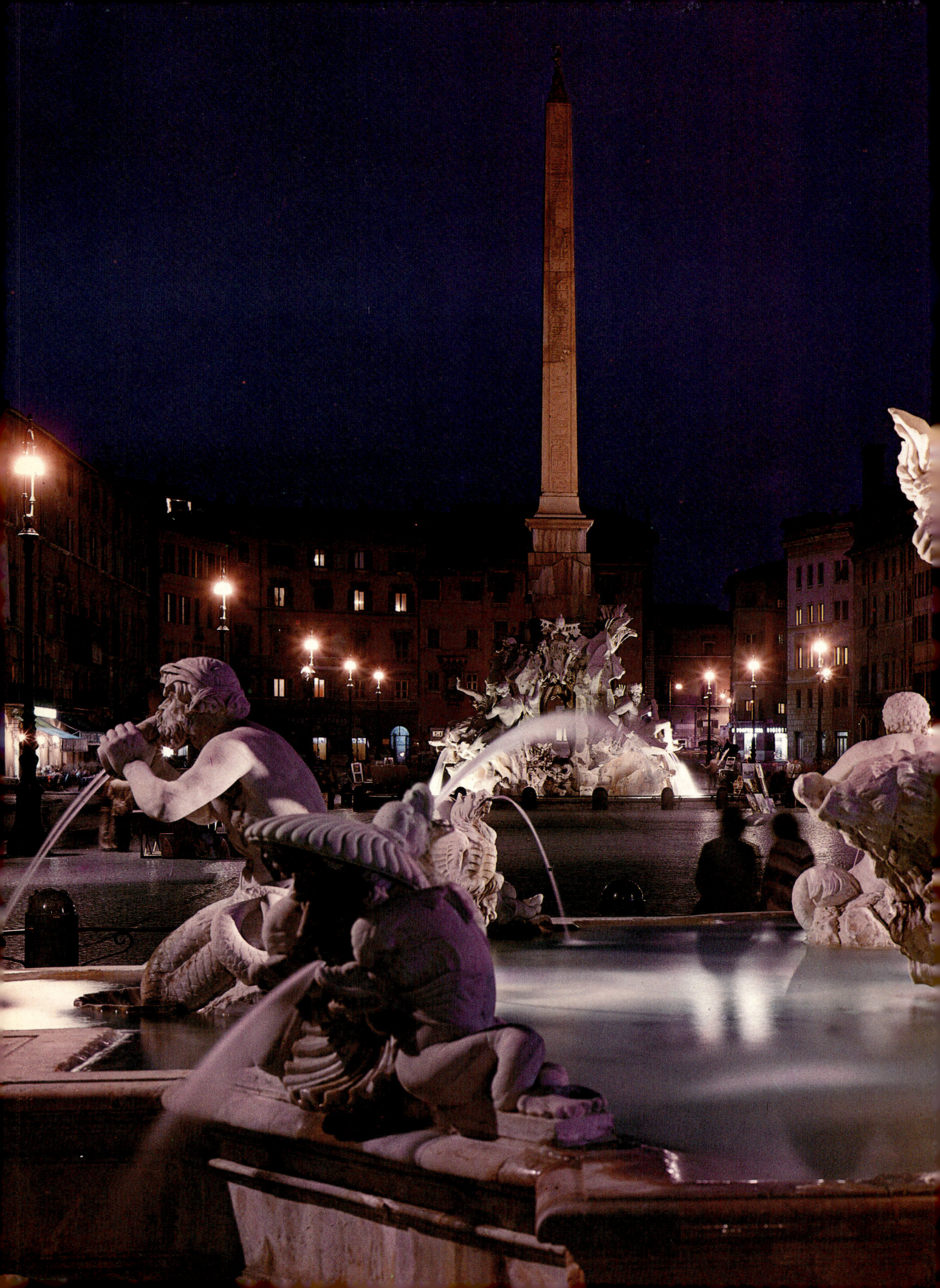

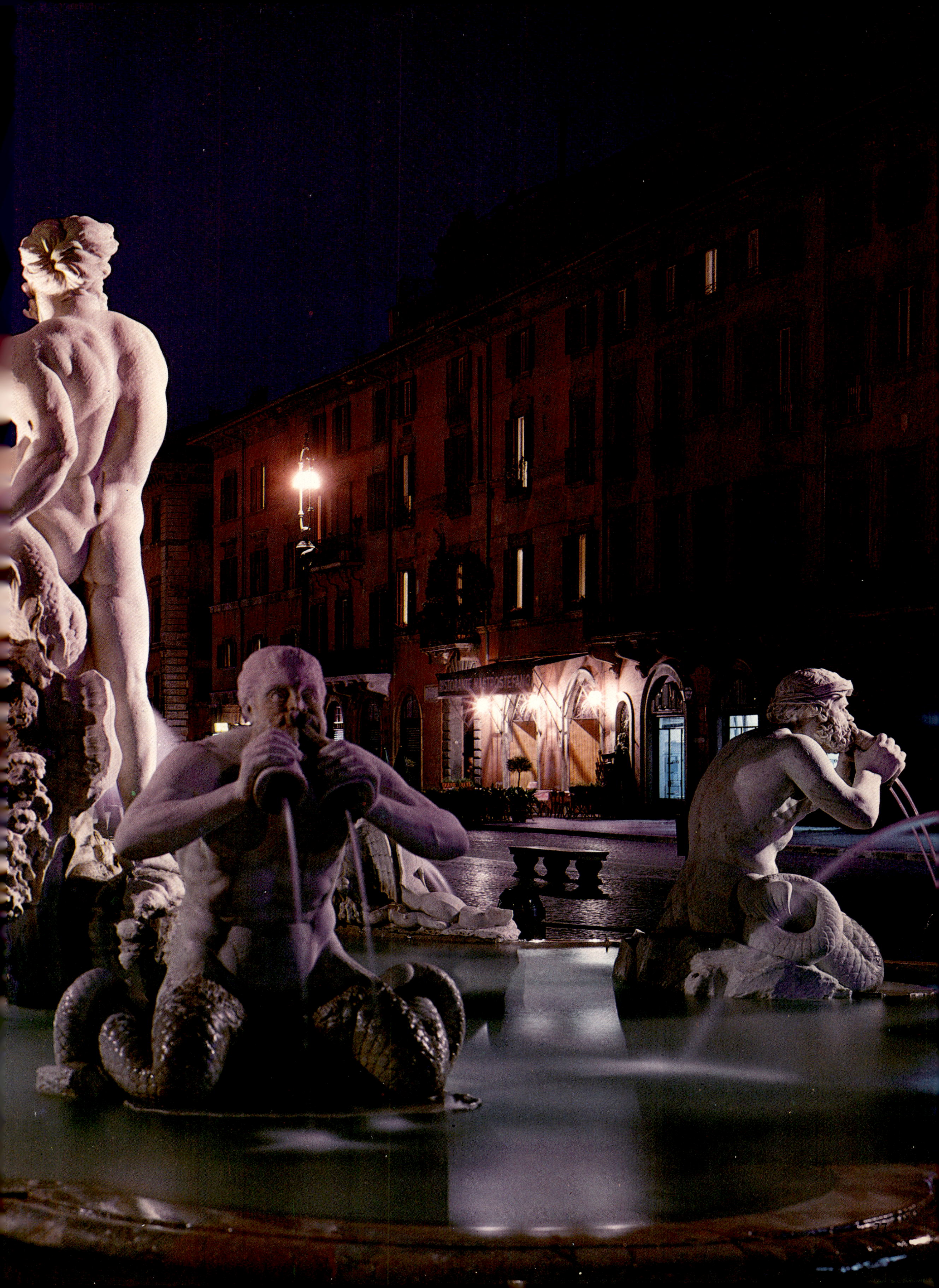
MASTROSTEFANO

78

Surrounded by a wealth of interesting buildings and familiar ristoranti right, *Navona Square, with its pretty, shuttered windows* below, *was once the center of sophisticated life in Baroque Rome. Within this spacious square can be seen three magnificent fountains – the Fountain of Neptune* above, *sited in the exedra, to the north, and shown overleaf with the massive central Fountain of the Rivers, and the Fountain of the Moor* left and previous page, *to the south of the square.*

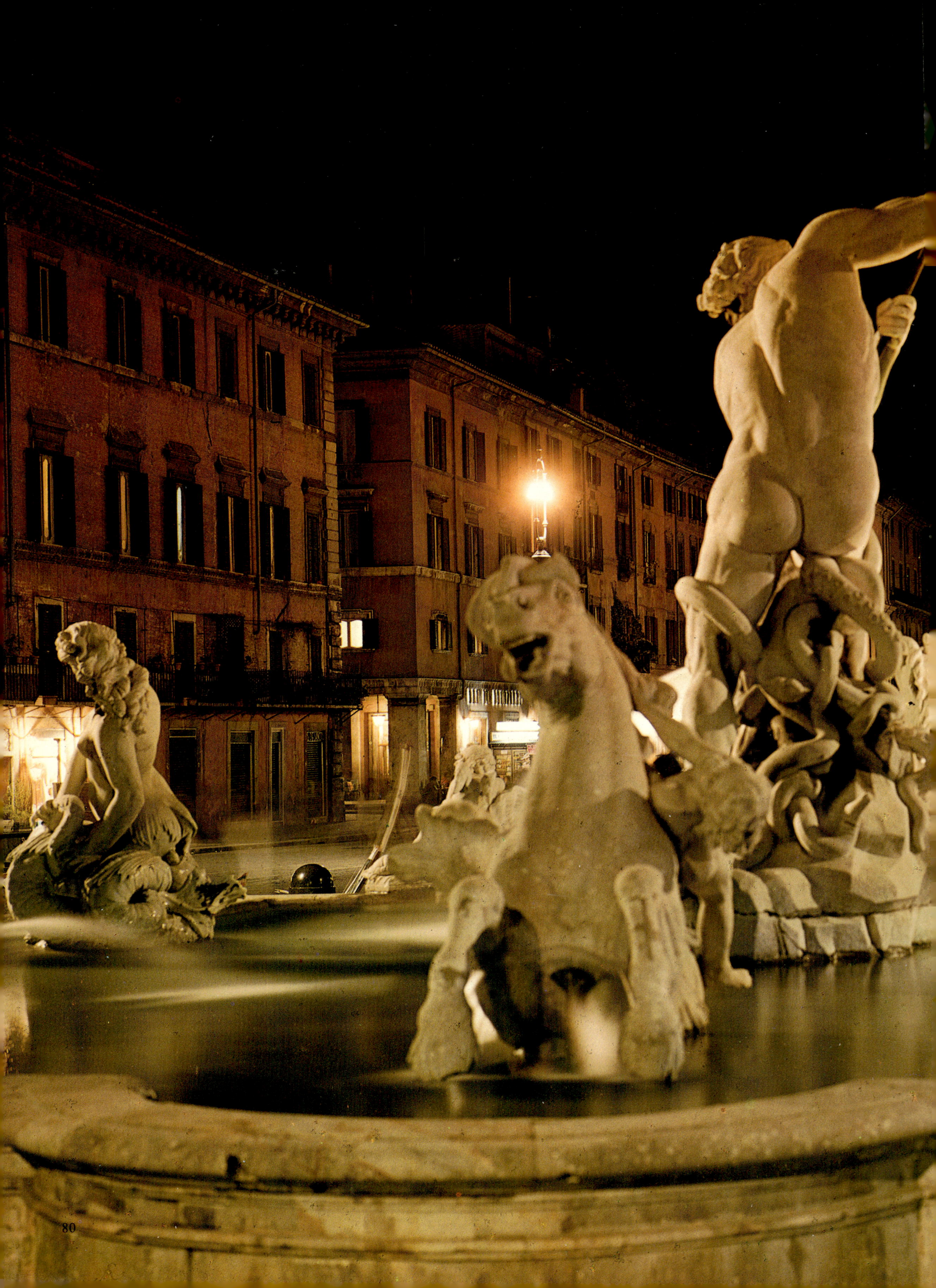

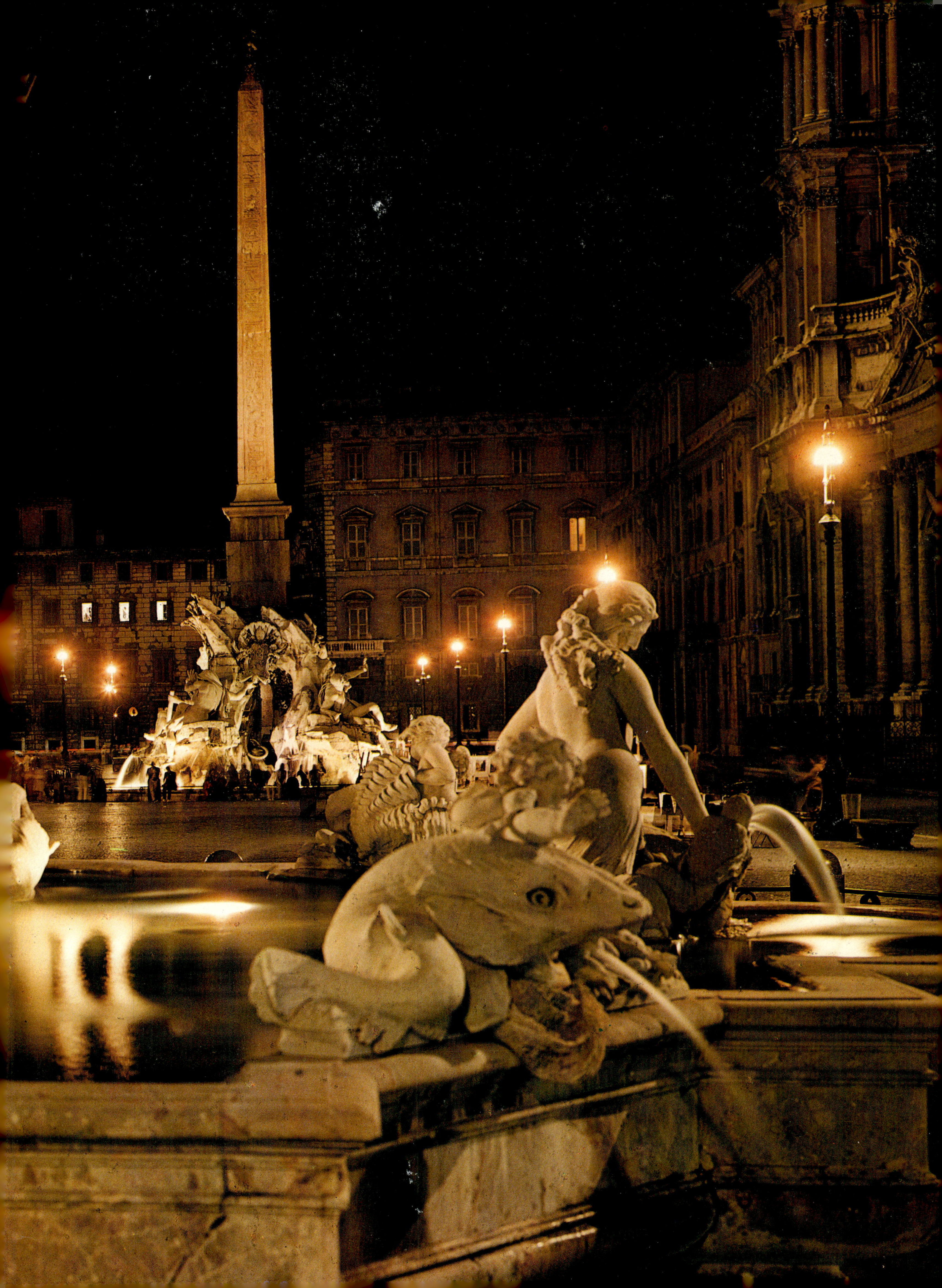

The old Roman street *right* and beautifully preserved monochrome mosaic at the Baths of Neptune *bottom left* can be seen in Ostia, the ancient Roman military base and port of republican Rome at the mouth of the Tiber, which was abandoned after the construction of Gregoriopolis (Ostia Antica) in the 9th century.

Built by the Emperor Hadrian in the 2nd century AD, Hadrian's Villa near Tivoli, with its lovely Canopus Canal *top left*, is filled with a wealth of ancient statuary and buildings *above, below and center left*, modelled on those of the classical Greek world.

Overleaf is shown the Capitoline Square at the summit of the smallest of Rome's seven hills.

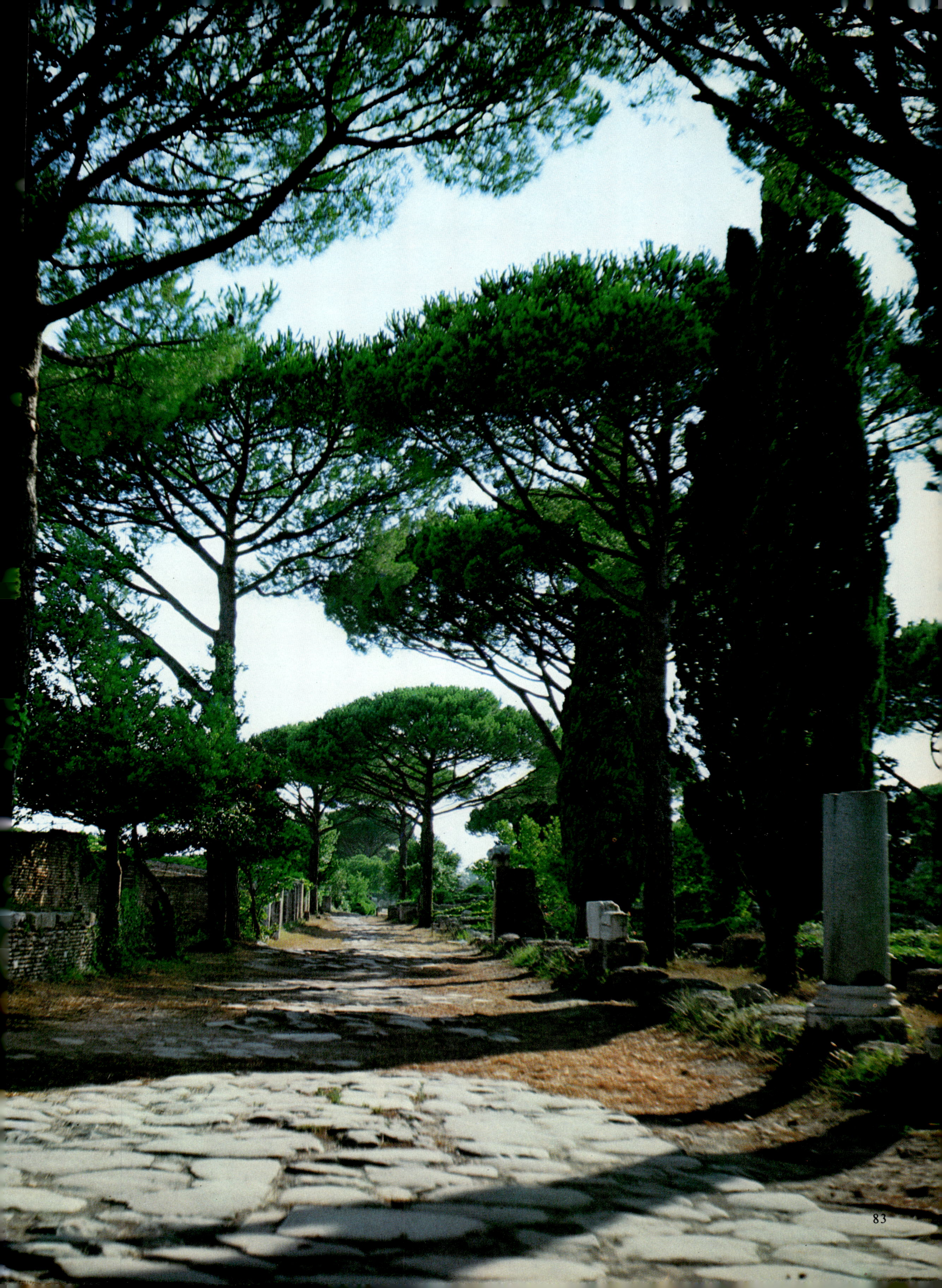

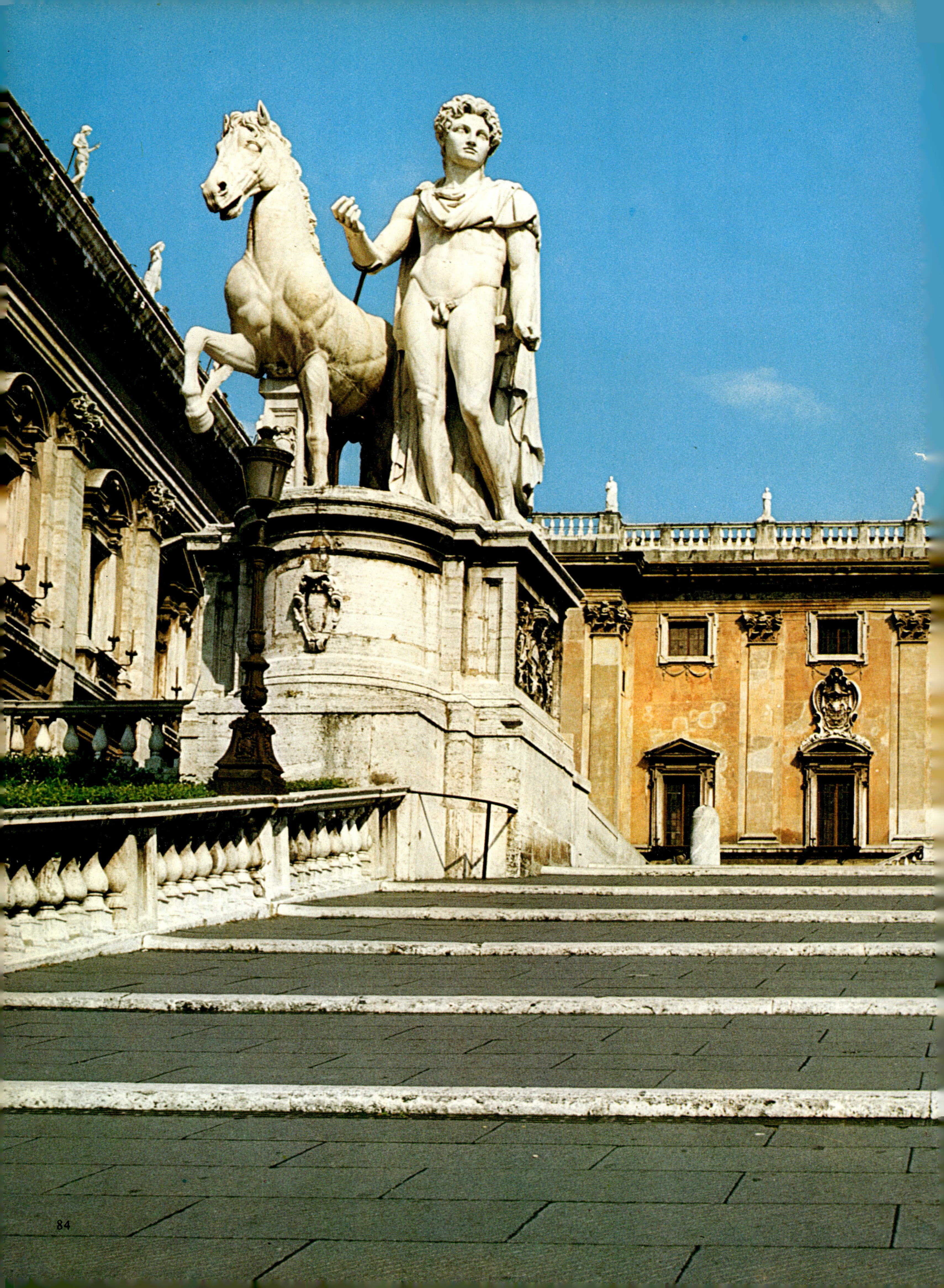

85

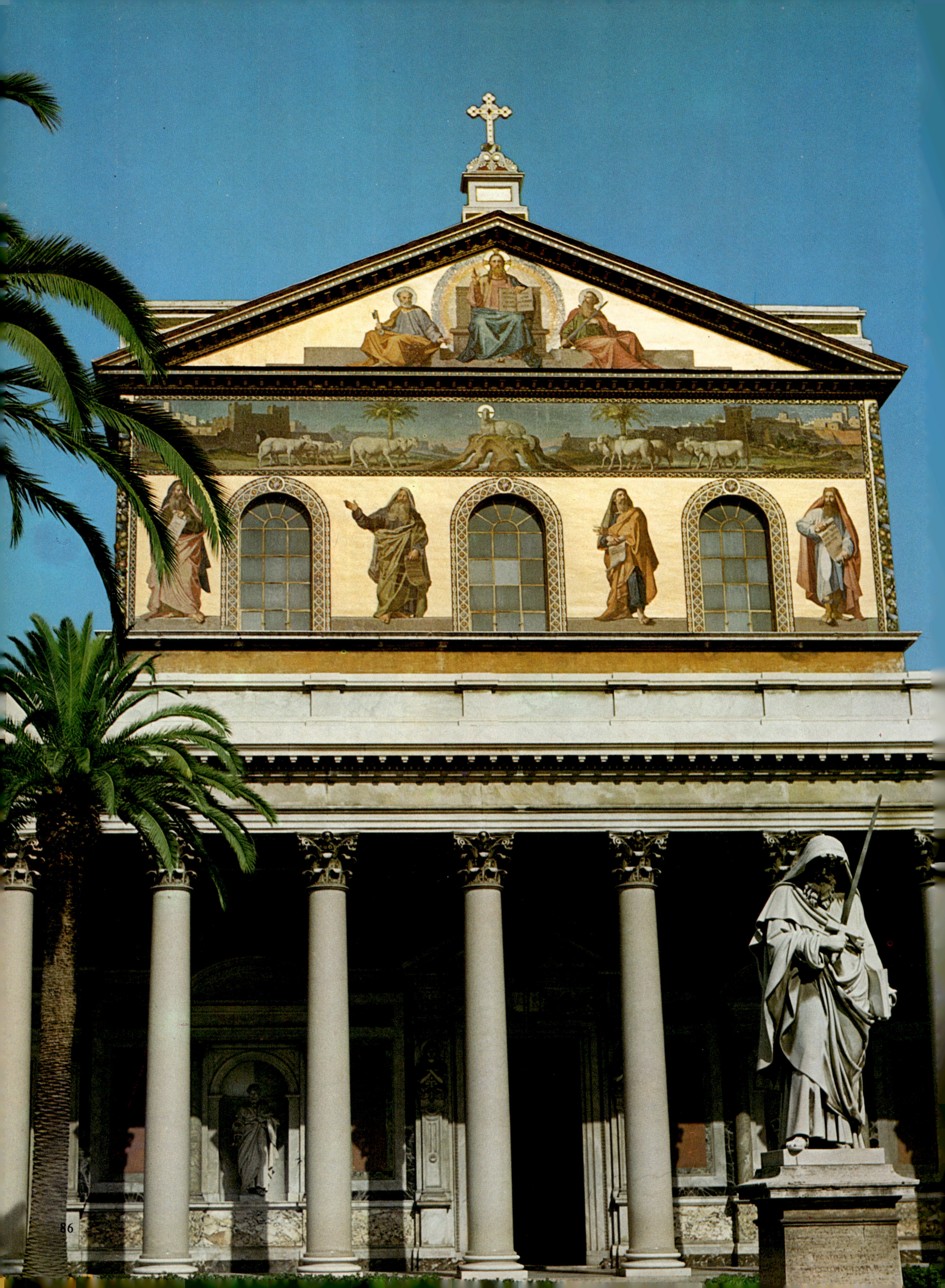

Magnificent churches and ancient temples, tranquil gardens and delightful fountains – Rome is filled with so many – yet each is unique, with a tireless beauty that never palls.

Left can be seen the lovely San Paolo furi le Mura (Basilica Ostiense), with its splendid cloister surmounted by an exquisite strip of mosaics; *above* the Forum Romano, majestic by night; *below* the Temple of Vesta, at the foot of the Capitoline Hill; *right* the charming gardens of the Villa Borghese, and overleaf the famous Trevi Fountain, built by Salvi and decorated by artists of Bernini's school.

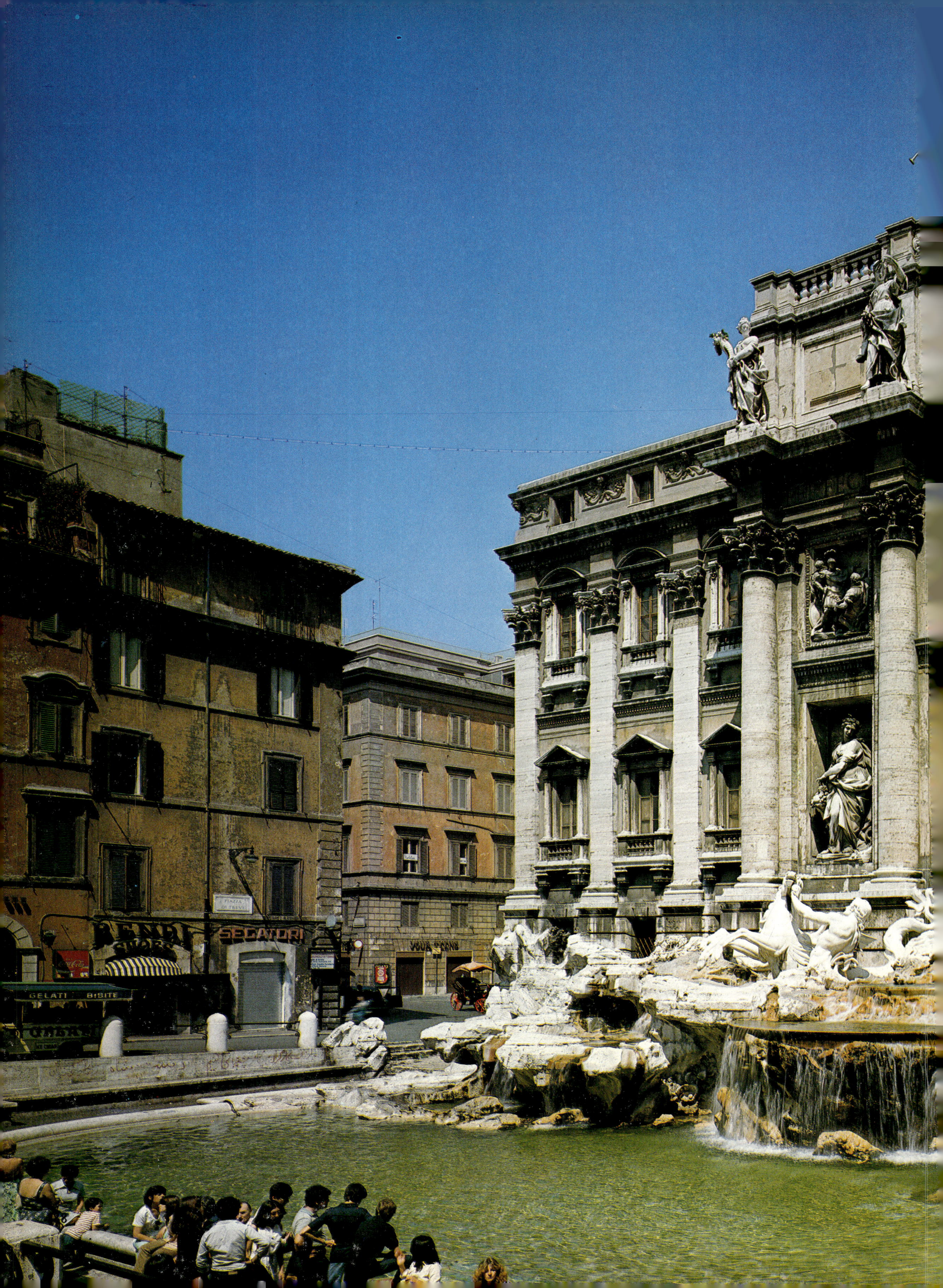
SEGATORI
GELATI

NS XII PONT MAX
AQVAM VIRGINEM
ALVBRITATE COMMENDATA
V MAGNIFICO ORNAVIT
MINI MDCCXXXV PONTIF VI
DICTVS XI

Considered to be one of the finest examples of the 'Italianate Style', the beautiful garden of the Villa d'Este is sited at Tivoli, some 30km from Rome. Set amid magnificently landscaped gardens with a wealth of fascinating fountains left, *the Villa below, was built in the 16th century by Pirro Ligorio and decorated by Muziano, Tempesta and Zuccari. Among its most noted fountains is the superb Organ's Fountain* right, *where an organ once played by means of the water jets, while* above *can be seen the impressive Hundred Fountain's Alley.*